PRAISE for Edmund Miller's Poetry

"*The Go-Go Boy Sonnets* is a celebration of the icons of gay New York. Miller pays homage to the indomitable spirit behind the pretty faces, displaying great affection and respect for his subjects as he captures the unique essence of each man. His word portraits, composed in sonnet form, are accompanied by biographical notes, and where appropriate. Translations into the subject's native tongue or other relevant languages. Where others tread only in broad, clichéd strokes, Miller crafts his sparkling verse with great specificity, revealing the shared humanity that lurks beneath the façade of this unconventional setting."

—Kim Volpe, *Long Island University Magazine*

The Go-Go Boy Sonnets is "a most enjoyable collection of poems that brings to mind another favorite book of poems, Masters's *Spoon River Anthology*. I was particularly delighted to find—in addition to the wit and eroticism—incisive and tender perceptions too. A uniquely pleasurable experience."

—Frank Kelly, Author of the poems *Growing Up Me*
and the play *Pageant*

On *Fucking Animals*: "Revealing and reveling in complexity within transparent simplicity .... Behind the playful, even zany, aura of many of the poems is a pragmatic sense of the melancholia that auras the cosmic appreciation of the beauty of young men from an adult manhood mind."

—Antler, Author of *Last Words*

Edmund Miller's gay poetry "has acquired a kind of legendary status. . . . The poems are witty, playful, and sometimes outrageous."

—Claude J. Summers, editor of *Gay and Lesbian Literary Heritage*

"Edmund Miller's poetry is gaily lyrical yet compact and intense. It rejoices in life's little details while evoking another world of artifice and ecstasy, laying poetics bare. Most surprisingly, in 'The Orange Challenge' he caresses the word not feasible to create the rhyme unattainable."

—Charles M. Kovich, Co-Author of *The Case of the Owl of Minerva* and other Father Shrader mysteries

"The slither-under-your-skin wit of *The Screwdriver's Apprentice* begins with the title and just becomes more irresistible, gloriously off-center, and alive as you make your way through these now-you-see-them-now-you . . . poems. I suppose the fact that they are hot, smart, and sensual is no more than we have come to respect from the brilliant Edmund Miller; these poems, however, seem to me to strike new depths of power, resulting in poems which are not only dazzling but moving, deeply so."

—James R. Kincaid, Author of *Annoying the Victorians, Erotic Innocence*, and such novels as *You Must Remember This* and *Lost*.

THE SCREWDRIVER'S APPRENTICE

Edmund Miller

BLUE LIGHT PRESS ❖ 1ST WORLD PUBLISHING

1ST WORLD
PUBLISHING

SAN FRANCISCO ❖ FAIRFIELD ❖ DELHI

1ST WORLD LIBRARY
PO Box 2211
Fairfield, IA 52556
www.1stworldpublishing.com

BLUE LIGHT PRESS
www.bluelightpress.com
Email: bluelightpress@aol.com

BOOK & COVER DESIGN
Melanie Gendron
www.melaniegendron.com

COVER ART
Cover collage illustration "Cartoon Love 1940-2010" by the author with *Pictures of Man Exercising* by Arthur Mount (AKA Monte Isom).

AUTHOR PHOTOGRAPH
Simon Van Booy

FIRST EDITION

Library of Congress Control Number: 2016963440

ISBN 9781421837710

Prior Publication:

Some of these poems have been published in journals:

"Muscles," "Beach Boy," "Indian Summer" (earlier version), and "They Always Leave Their Undershirts" (earlier version) in *Mouth of the Dragon*; "Stolen Moments" (earlier version) in *Indigo*; "Big Musical Number" (earlier version, prize poem) in *Scoop*; "Learner's Permit" (earlier version) in *Duck*; "Commemorative" (earlier version) in *Sun Tan*; "Australian Rules" (earlier version) in *Bay Windows*; "Double Dactyls" segment "Cut Up" in *The Missouri English Bulletin*; "The Orange Challenge" in *Vice*; "A Valediction of Our Route on the Map" (earlier version) in *Soundings*, and "Got It" and "Assiduities" (earlier version) in *The PPA Literary Review*.

Some have been published in anthologies:

"Make Me." *Seduced . . . May They Lead Us into Temptation.*
    Ed. John Patrick. Sarasota: STARBooks, 1993.
"Voyeur." *Runaways/Kid Stuff.*
    Ed. John Patrick. Sarasota: STARBooks, 1994.
"In the Porno Theater." *The Badboy Book of Erotic Poetry.*
    Ed. David Laurents. New York: Masquerade, 1995.
"Social Intercourse." *Poetic Voices without Borders 2.*
    Ed. Robert L. Giron. Arlington: Gival, 2009.

Some have been published in the following of the author's chapbooks and fiction:

Slapshots à Go Go, A Rider of Currents, The Happiness Cure, Muttonchop Laughter, I Shouldn't Have Waited, and the short story collection *Night Times.*

The manuscript for this work won honorable mention as a Gival Prize book.

For Anderson Weekes,
my most enthusiastic reader

Contents

GOT IT

Careening through supermarket streets
skating on bluejean wheels
to the bells of romance,
straightening a fancy tie
against its paisley sky,
the living boy
wings by
with dance.

BACK SEAT

Though blushing in the clinches
I am chewing at a steady pace
and reposing in the web of it,
not making all that big a deal of it.
There's no point in knocking myself out,
I feel,
just to keep a metaphor
alive.
And you needn't bother flinching,
and who can touch me really?
I have dimples on my butt.

WORKOUT ROUTINE

1.   The naked narcissist,
          redundant thumbs in his beltloops,
          goes around with his top down,
          running in place,
          ready for more.
          I collapse on the sofa
          in my exercise suit—
          calves swollen.

2.   There's a mole behind
          just by the roll-up
          of his jockstrap.
          Streaks of sweat
          run down
          his cheeks,
          his chest,
          my soul.

LUNCH

Arched back on boardwalk
High above the footmarks,
Beyond the reach
Of the beach,
He scans the horizon,
Dreamy
In a bikini
With a salami
Dazzling the birds
In the sand.

ACTOR

1.   The actor leans against the wall,
        awaiting compliments.
        There's a scar on his face,
        but it's hiding coy
        in the beauty
        of the side
        of his nose.

2.   It dates without doubt
        from a dueling German romance
        or a set-to on the Orient Express
        or a Renaissance—
        somewhere.
        And he has papers
        to prove it.

3.   The boy in him is breaking
        through the spaces in his mind
        into mirror writing
        of an infant kind
        that yet can swell with music
        and somehow come out fighting
        from the distended jaws of time.

LEARNER'S PERMIT

For Monroe, in graduate school

I saw him in the grocery store.
bedecked in gas-station grime
buying bread and cheese.
His hips
slung very low.
He had a tiny tattoo
on his neck.
I kept looking inside
the corner
of his wraparound darkglasses
as he checked out ahead of me
and left.

BIG MUSICAL NUMBER

Why is this chorus boy unlike
All other chorus boys?
Or is he? Well, he's
built big.
I mean behind.
But in the chest and shoulders too. Yes,
for all the rippling cross the belly,
unaffected, happy, he's
for a change fleshy
quivering live. But even that
isn't all of it for me,
seeing stars.
It's that he really means his part
and dances with his heart
and beats out a little time
when he's standing on the side
and flashes out a smile,
panting
down between the rows.

PLAYROOM

I don't really know that I want it
but boy do I like to play at it.
Dawdling in the sunsheets
for everyone to see
I'm inwardly sailing to toychests
and thumping my little tin drum
awaiting a hard-core red wagon.
So every other day at least
I get out the coloring book
to page with my past.
But of course my crimson crayon
never strays outside the lines.

WATER BOY

I'm keeping this under my beachburnt brows,
but, my, haven't you gotten to be the big boy,
your tatoos all rippling,
your walk a shore leave?
And wouldn't I like to have seen it all happen
under the waterblue eyes
of some jade-green marine
or sailor's-haven buddy
since lost at sea?
And don't you remember
I did like you really?
This is no new sudden thing. And
where are you off to? And
why am I asking?

BEACH BOY

To this beach
he lays his claim
as he wraps himself up
in miniature muscled arms,
slipping the fingers under,
and not on one side only
in a natural crisscross fold,
but on both sides together,
displaying the biceps,
embracing himself.
Then with dusk
he falls to sleep,
rolling over,
his dancing slope
hard regardless.
And the miniature muscled arms
spread wide their curly armpits
and lie yawning
on the beach.

VOYEUR

Creeping to the window
shrouded in the artificial night
of all indoors,
I spy the little boy next door
angling on the sofa
in his underdrawers, there
before him his bated brother,
the bigger boy next door,
equally next to naked,
flailing his arms in exercise
fore and aft
and checking periodically his chest
for the tell-tale swollen bruises
of success.

SANDY

The sand was blond and Apollonian.
I was dreaming at muscle beach
(Because looking around there's too easy)
About gold conceited things and
How you always fall for the type
Fashionable then
When you were—when
In the blondhood of his own interminable time
One of them
Stepped out of the Aegean
And washed philosophically up on the beach.
There were banks of blonds everywhere
But only one
Had the necessary mole at the small of the back.
"Well, you must be the purely classical lover,"
He said, "and I the Greek god."
And then I knew:
This must be the blond.

LIDS

Like an East German,
sandy-haired on the train, he
sleeps without his eyes closed,
a California rosé wine
fermenting in the canyons
of his parted lips.

REMEMBERED MOMENTS

1.   The sign I almost read
by dim daylight
in some headshop vestibule,
says, oh, "Do not handle candle."

2.   And what was all he said
that some same night,
yearning to play pool?
Was it only "I'm after the next guy"?

3.   Something borrowed, something untrue,
Sweating with night intensity,
Sticks to me like a postage stamp
Sending me all its glue.

4.   They always forget
Their undershirts:
The smell of vaseline
and jelly bean.

INTRO TO FICTION

His body left behind,
He bows his head in worship
At the exam I give. Just then
His body at ease is mine
As I am freed to watch
At last. And the spark of life
I see remains. His jeans,
With a certain interest,
A sure utility,
have passed beyond threadbare
Into deep reality.
There is a hole,
Of substantial size,
Its edges raw, frayed, bleached
To a fine point of whiteness,
Right at the crotch—
A little to the rear perhaps.
And all the interior blazes
Passionate red. I get this peek
Within because he slouches
And lets his legs go wide and limp,
Putting his own furnace of fictions
Out of mind and
Giving himself over to me
Wholeheartedly,
Giving himself over
To my fiction.

MARBLES

For Brig from high school

I no longer remember
the Gregorian chant with incense
in altar-boy days
hoofbeats racing through bread-and-cheese hollows
butterflies in the attic
silently singing to escape
the tea ceremony on the beach
with white umbrellas.
I don't know

How many basketball games there were
Or whether you ever cried.
I don't know when you gave up football
if you had to marry
what you sold your soul for.
I don't even know
whether it was glass or
when you're coming home.
Or what you're coming home for.

STOLEN MOMENTS

1.   Nightly on an indigo shore
    in the space of dreams
    a vicarious tool works at play. Then
    someone takes up the vegetarian guitar
    and negligent strums away
    till the dawn is creamy with stars.

2.   "Shoot for the sky,"
    the masked man suggested,
    "and empty your pockets
    on the piano." But the boy
    spoke only
    French.

THE VERY MAN

For Steve on my first real teaching position

Torso-shirted
Cream-centered sin,
He stands there
Dreamy, loose.
By rocks smoothed with the salt of waves,
He stands there
Happy, private, away
In an attic,
Forgetting
Yesterdays.
He stands there,
The silky inside of him
Like bitter cocoa
Because I want it that way.
There's nothing there now.
Nothing much at all remains.
Yet he stands there.
And every day, all day
The smell of him.

DITHYRAMB

The trapezoidal cadence of his hips
as he merely walks along
bowed but active
across the ice
and out of the picture
playing froggy hump with reality
and marrying outside his own sex.

His muscles taste like strawberry wine
silky and smooth and uncertain
holding back the brawn
as the hard outline
of him in the dark leafy and sleepy
with fingers touching soft times past
but bringing fair weather never and always.

TOMMY GUN

For Thom Gunn

Studly, weatherbeaten,
he hardly moves at all
when he dances;
he hardly dances at all
when he sings.

MOMENTS

A rainbow reaches the seagulls.
Your tobacco smells so delicious.
He has eyelashes to his ankles.
And everything Greek is religious.

DAY DREAM

Thumping Kansas—
clean and stormy—
craves
the unseasonable
the unleashed,
the unwashed
Novembers of ladhood,
transparent.
I remember
an unchained boy.
Time was
a game we played—
lust incipient,
and then
cool it
at home,
observing,
lost in the private,
smooth,
eucharistic
void
beyond the stars.

COMPETITION

Here we are competing for the same
thing.
Is there any question
who'll get it?
All he has on his side is
youth—
oh, and beauty.

FALL AND SPRING

With black curls
all over his forehead
and suitably singing eyes,
He rollerblades away
the spongy day.
He's a springy boy.
But what did I think of
yesterday floating home?
Alive with artificial flowers,
nosegay crotches
stare at concrete,
breeding worms
and growing bold.
And satyrs wearing
virgins in their hair
wet the walks with September
and tarnish
in the cold.
Till then his bloom appears,
and we're up to our ears
in music.

PIE

A finger-licking boy
with shocking black eyes
and thighs black and blue
and an applesauce ass
not noticeably picking his nose
is all I ask.

SPRUNG

In the fancy spring
when a young man's
worm turns
every ass-station pumpboy
agreeably
offers a fill-up.

MERCILESSLY

He might be
pretending to be
interested in
no one but me.
Then again
he might not be.

TRYST

Is he holding me up?
Or am I holding him?

He hit me.
He took it.

I took it.
He hates himself.

I loved it.
I hated it.

He forgot.
He forgot himself.

I wouldn't let him.
I couldn't stop him.

He won't let me go.
He won't let me come.

Is this a poem?
Isn't this a poem?

NAKED

I want to be nearing him
hearing him
talk
watching him
walk
gawking.
He takes me
seriously he takes me.
New ideas knock up my mind
questions not answers
his not mine.
Mined.

GAME

Tackling a tackle in the hall. What gall!
Gotcha!
Grabbing a guy round the middle part with art.
Gotcha!
Playing for laughs in a riot of May. Hey!
Gotcha!
Gaming away in a gamy way. Say!
Gotcha!
Spying his eying from the corner of the mind. Mind.
Gotcha.

ASSIDUITIES

1.   He's trampling the air
with his mass and
hairychesting so much he
can't even close my corded jacket.
Passing by, he's pink
like the strapping backside
of true love.

2.   The father is a blond
with a Fu Manchu mustache
and shoulders out to Arkansas
and many buttons missing.
Passing by, he's a bedroom blond
with roving hips.
And baby is a boy.

3.   His white-chocolate poetry
melts in my mind, a sweet
disagreeable mess.
His talk pursues me to the showers
and opens up my dreams at night
with paperweight concretions.
An oil lamp burns in his body.

4.   I reach for the light.
But I singe my fingers.
And now there's ice
in his eyes.

DUNGAREE

My basket is bursting with goodies.
I'm aging as fast as I can.
My studded mind
leaps flame,
abandons game.
My hairy guts
loiter with lubricant
listen for cuts.
I dip into his pockets and
licking all the lint out
smell the skin burn.

COCKEYED

There are poisonous corded places
in his face.
But there are cheeky rubbery dimples
too.
It's such a smoking bony face.
There are bristles everywhere.
Yet there's dancing.
With tears in his eyes,
I cry.

MAKE ME

The bulging-down-below
all-crowded-around
all-corduroy youth
with the animal name
has his ass hanging out
on the everready.
And on the playing field.
All the boys love it—
the way he can do it,
the way he can make it,
the way he can take it.
But what's a body for,
gnawing away?
Is it just that?

THE DRIFT

it hasn't rained here in years
if it would I'd be happy
or sappy or would I
the big little boys put-put-put
their muffled lives away
beers but no tears
peerless among their peers
it hasn't snowed here in years
the lock of his pubic hair
zipped away in a locket somewhere
on a dare I feel the skin of a peach
drying out, drying out, gone away
grass, alas, brings no pass
snow job, no job
it hasn't stormed here in years
sulking, sucking
by yourself your thumb
waiting for the weather
to change
or rearrange
slipping ticking timeouts
that haven't hailed from here in years
in our everyday, womb-a-day
life

AUSTRALIAN RULES

Home for Christmas and looking
for trouble, I spend the idle hours
while the sugarplums are sleeping
spinning the remote control
on my brother's supercolossal,
mythopoetic, cable-connected T.V.

He has all those extra channels—
that one from Atlanta
you can never find in the listings
and the fancy ones
you pay extra for
when you have money to burn.

But you keep spinning and spinning.
Nobody ever saw these first-run movies
out in the real world of head-on collisions.
There aren't even any commercials
disengaging you for drift-away.
Even the sex channel is painless.

But Sportschannel, oh you kid!
Who would have thought it? Up
between the antiseptic tennis
and the hoopla of the big-time games,
Australian Rules Football
lacerates the screen.

Dressed for a genteel game of soccer,
red-gold giants baked raw by the sun
explode—with the violence of Rugby—
like fireworks on the Queen's birthday
and thunder across the field getting dirty
down under as they hunger for the goal.

Yet nobody lies bleeding
or gets carried off the field.
And all this without a helmet—
without a kneepad,
without a mask,
without a cup.

TAXI

Big black taxi man
fingers bigger than most men's
things
sensuous girl-
crazy
lecherous alert
watching the sledders
the sweaters
the swells
sliding across the street.

MARRIAGE

As he grows slowly bald
And I get gray,
We live our pretty life away
In artificial youth and harmony
Because I loved him once
And he liked me.

ICING

Life takes me by wild surprise
and suddenly it's raining
and suddenly it's not.
And the birds fly back to Kansas
freshly cut out for it.
I can feel blushing Missouri
In my small bones.
I let you know me
and it doesn't really hurt.
And I don't have any vices
and everybody cares.
But then all alone
even touching stone
I blush.

SUMMER SUN

1.   Stolen nipples
       Listing,
       Suntanned,
       Southward
       Toward
       Listening
       Hairy
       Lifeholes.

2.   The freckled tortoiseshell trousers.
     The lingering crotchety eggshell fingers
            Raking through hair.
     The watermarked complex silk
            Complexion, abused, burning.
     The body,
            Red,
            Hairlike,

        But sweaty sweet at home there,
     Tasting today's play,
     Reviving
            The airy lawn,
            The greasy air,
            The stunning sun.

SAILOR

A taut deck of shipshape hip
　　Sloping up from sunrise somewhere.
A downturn from a heady lip.
　　　The blondness of him everywhere
　　　With his waxing, frosty bodyhair.
With his sunsetty, unsettling eyes
He frowns and clowns and lies
And makes a curling, fantasy trip.

　　　Into port and out again to sea so fast—
And lasting—
　　　With the sweet and fluted turnaround
　　　And grinning, chinny sailaway
Off into the once again once only body dream past recall,
Off into the hardheaded hardbody past recall, and all.

INDIAN SUMMER

You looked back, and an Indian laughed
In dandelion thighs:
Little Beauty, Little Craft,
With gray occasional rawhide eyes
And dogwood joy—
A warpainted red natural roundabout boy.

His brave black brush-brows
Set my wampum afire;
His grand indifference cows
Me as the hardness of my dreams
Loincloths what seems
And lights with a cold glowing gold my vernal desire.
But no pow wow—
Anyhow, not now.

THE BEAUTY OF A MALE MODEL FADES

About his symmetry, the chief thing I'll
       Recall is the nose unmoved by mouth in pout
       While little crows' feet stepped out
To share the boldness of his smile
And resonate the vibrancy of lips
       Across a Devonshire cream complexion
       With just one beauty mark to its perfection.
Jerked to a climax, my attention flips

Into present. Bold lips go down on rock;
       Then—throbbing up—I reinflate and, now
       Careless of the beauty all around, plough
Till he at last the Lethean liplock
       Unlooses, letting him demonstrate how
A *GQ* face recreams with aftershock.

IN THE PORNO THEATER

Now suddenly everyone's hot to be
      Tight with me. Why, I'm all aglow tonight!
      At least I must be doing one thing right
Since sitting rub-a-dub snug beside me
Is a guy who's passed me up many times.
      Yet he lunges for my little nipper,
      Fingering my crotch, oping my zipper,
Hoisting me erect, setting off my chimes.

But all the while this expert boldly ducks,
I long for something worth the whole nine bucks
Paid at the door. At last I catch the eye
Of a better guy, eye-lashed, standing by.
      Groping this hunk enables me to shoot,
      But, then, I find he gives my hand the boot.

SOCIAL INTERCOURSE

Revealing unexpected social lives,
All the title holders among the men
Fall in with courtly escort duty when
The body builders bring along their wives:
Because they check male bonding at the door,
Like Old Regime French aristocracy
They swap spouses without hypocrisy.
The guys—who clearly aren't out to score—
Exercise conversational passion
To share their small talk like nobility
And—pumped beyond the familiar fashion
Shaping suburban class mobility—
Surprise with relaxed elasticity,
Not uxorious domesticity.

NEAR MISS

For Chellis Fetzer

Clean and sober
And all alone
At the Roxy,
About to accost
Porn star Jake Andrews
To tell him how much
I admire his work,
I am myself accosted
By a drag queen
Done up in white
With such improbable good taste
That just for a moment
I think she's a woman.

LEARNING FROM LAP DANCERS

For Rico Brazil at the Show Palace

Earlier in the evening
sitting in the lobby
in all his spandex glory,
so not-on-the-hustle,
so above-it-all,
he looked right through me.
I didn't even know for sure
that he was part of the show.
But then he did get up
to take a turn on stage and off stage,
and when he made his rounds
and lap-danced over to me,
I could see he could see
that I wanted him
just from the way I was touching.
I tipped him. I tipped him again,
and then he asked,
"Would you like a private show?"
I had the presence of mind
to want to know his price.
But at just twenty dollars,
I could not but choose. Semi-private
in a back row, I began licking
his chest—sweet at the belly button,
scented with basil higher up.
I ran hands over his body,
saluting his hardness

with fingertips
When I opened myself
to woodwork invitation,
even half-hard
he filled me up.
But then he unzipped me too
and began jacking my hammer.
When in my body worship
almost inadvertently
I glanced a nipple,
with sudden urgency
he sprang to full attention.
"So that's the key," I thought,
"to ecstasy." So I flicked away
at nipples, and licked away,
paying his price. Just
to finish up I had him turn around
and licked sweat off the hard behind.
Neither of us came to it. Leaving
me nonetheless light-headed,
he seemed astonished
by a ten dollar tip.
Such open surprise
was cheap at the price,
for I saw in a trice
the point of paying twice:
the inaccessible stud
is really yours at last
when he comes to see smiling
as part of the job.

LEARNING FROM LESBIANS

At a tense domestic moment
in Susan Dreher's mystery *Something Shady*,
the Lesbian detective Stoner McTavish
stalks severely from the bedroom,
leaving there her lifemate,
sitting on the bed,
stewing in frustration,
picking away
at her duvet.
I fretted over the passage,
contemplated byways of curious anatomy
and conjured up conundrums
of an apparatus shipped in secret
all the way from France.
Sinking in perplexity,
at last I looked it up—
to learn a hoary female truth
the butchest Lesbian will know:
the lifemate twiddling her thumbs
was worrying the fluffy nap
of a frilly coverlet,
her only bedroom comforter.

DUO

One is big,
And one is little.
One is all muscle in a leather vest,
And one looks slight even in a puffy-sleeved shirt.
One has hair that's too long
And too black,
And one has hair too platinum blond
Clipped too high on the sides.
One has a big round butt,
And one has a flat little no-butt-to-speak-of.
One walks all bow-legged,
And one walks all swish.
But it's true
What they say
About couples
Growing to look alike:
In profile
They have the same
Nose.

NOTED IN PASSING

Standing next to me
Has to be
The perfect guy.
He's nice and short
But with very broad shoulders
And no waist at all.
If he deviates
For the classical ideal
It's just by the length
Of his eyelashes—
Way too long—
And the jet blackness
Of his hair.
Which is groomed
Meticulously—
Short enough
To leave full face in view
But not hacked away—
And so obedient
It falls into place
With soft naturalness.
He wears
A Jocko shirt—
With logo imprinted
Discreetly on the collar
In the back.
For jewelry he sports
Just two tiny studs
In his left ear—
And (What's this?)

A plain gold ring
Also rising in the east.
But now that I take a better look—
Peeking inside from behind—
I see he's tucked
That stylish Jocko shirt
Down into designer briefs.
So he wouldn't do
Anyway,
I make a quick getaway.

LAP DANCE

Sitting at the bar
With my stool turned to the side
So I can scope the room,
I receive a casual visitor
Who leans across my lap
To place an order.
I run my fingers down his back
Tracking the line
Of the spine.
He offers me no comment
But greets a dear old friend
Discovered sitting just beyond
On the other side from me.
They chat
And keep at that
For quite some time.
So I redetect the spinal line,
Resume my delicate tracery.
We continue
Along our respective paths
For ten minutes or fifteen.
Then he turns ferocious queen
And asks how I dare take such
Liberties.
"Usually," I say,
"When someone spends so long
Sprawled across my lap,
He wants, instead of yanking,
A long hard spanking,
But I don't sing that rap."

A VALEDICTION OF OUR ROUTE ON THE MAP

Religiously impassioned from above,
Donne's stiff twin compasses don't resonate.
Golden circles miss how we separate,
Unchained, without a spinning circled love.
Yet we love as compasses when parted
(Valentine's Day) transcontinentally,
For we mark the map sentimentally
With design to soothe the broken-hearted.

From where we two stand erect at the train,
I spiral the Archimedean track.
But you, rooted firmly south, pull me back.
So I rush my business, fast for you, plane
Swiftly, then curve round, impatient in air,
Drawing home a paper heart ever there.

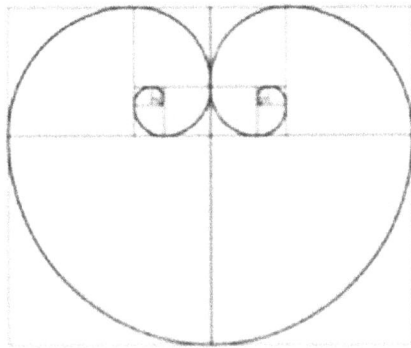

MOONSTRUCK

Can my mooning eyes
be such a surprise?
Honestly
there's just mooncalf me.
The depths you can sound
you can see.
And my flexing muscles
can't hide
the white flesh creeping inside
by the milklight
of the moon.

FOUND POETRY

1.   In Bed:

    TO OPEN
    · SLIT OPEN ON THREE SIDES
    · PULL BACK WRAPPER AND REMOVE SLICES
    · REPLACE WRAPPER FOR PROTECTION

2.   Elsewhere

    A long lasting, crisp,
    exhilarating scent that
    gives a man the
    physical advantage.
    Well placed, it can be
    your most effective
    weapon.

SPURS

When I look at him
through my black eyes
I see blood on his hands
and melting wax
there in the dark.
There's a metal stud
on his zipper hook.
He wears black leather pants
to bed
and doesn't take his boots off.
And there's a whip on the nighttable
but no lubricants.
Oh it's true there's a scar
on his forehead
where the beltbuckle hit
and blood of his own
in the hair
on his chest.
But by his light
he's all right.
He doesn't fight.
It's just me.

OPEN OVERCOAT IN THE SNOW

I stare into sunglass mirrors.
what am I doing? Why
I'm writing a poem. If
I agree to put you in it
will you stay here
at least a little while?
The flapping back
of the coat against his thigh
walking on by.

SMASHING

You seem to see that
open coated I'm a hairy bear
whether I do or don't
wear under there underwear
oh I can smile back at you
and enjoy it too
like open air and exercise
like coming in first
and winning the prize
because I can
you've heard
rip things off
the walls and smash
things in and work out my
frustration
though I never touch people
you're sure.

OVER

My little lapse of violence
sapped away my nerve.
My body is heated and thawing
my soft mind congeals.
I see your music everywhere
I find you listening when I'm alone.
I'm waiting for it to start over—
I'm waiting for you to come back.
You're here with me always—
you're here with me anyway.
Speak to my dark frightened quiet—
lie down with my lap for your pillow.

MOCK

Leaning forward as he walks
or crossing his legs as he sits and talks
crossing the room in a bound
with a bang
or slouching and thinking
or thinking out loud
standing out in a crowd
gnawing his cigarette
shrugging his dimples
with bright bones
he lights up the day.

BRIGHTPATH

Sitting there
in your surf's up hair
beside yourself
like a grinning elf
you have a lot of fun
screwing up the works
and taking all the blame.
Then one day you want to run
and hide from all the shame.
Crying blind
you have to yell,
"What the hell!"
(in your mind).

CASUAL

"Baby yourself," he says
indolently
and I feel the blood in my veins
my mind my muscle
soak it up.
Or "Come again," he says
and I do
and he does
and we do.
But "See you," he says.
I mean it.
So does he?

EYE

With windowshade eyeshades
up and spinning in the
memorable morn
any moment now
he has green honest eyes
so they don't really glow
in my dark.

MUSCLES

I spend a lot of time
pretending not to be
thinking all the time
only about me.
These hard muscles
all over you see
are only the way
I want to be.
And I wish there were
someone to tell
to taste it
to touch the inside.

INTERCOURSE

1   Have you been sleeping?
       Did I just wake you?
       Did you want me to do that?
       Am I sure that I love you?

2   Have you quite finished?
       Are you beginning?
       Shall we say stop now?
       Who's to say no?

3   Aren't you laughing?
       Do we have tomorrow?
       Isn't this lovely?
       Do we have all day?

4   Will we want later?
       Will we get more?
       Will the time come?
       Have you forgotten?

5   Aren't we waiting?
       Is it all over?
       Aren't you sorry?
       When do I start?

SNAPSHOT

With a line in some debt to Martin Beller

Your picture's just fallen to the floor
denting its fake gold frame,
and now the glass is broken,
and I can see you only there
behind the cracks again. Really
I'd forgotten all about it. But
it seems it had been resting
on my desk since you left
whenever it was that that was.

You are smiling in the picture—
that is always a mistake—
ever so forever and ever it seems.
Your smile brings back no memory
nor touches any loss though
your picture is here before me now
underfoot. Yet I think of poor you,
for so well as I can recall
you forgot ever to ask for mine.

DOUBLE DACTYLS

1.   AWASH

Dickery-Daiqueri,
Jim Douglas Morrison,
Straining for artistry,
Took to the brew

After his music's ly-
Surgic acidity
Chemopoetically
Broke him on through.

2.   CUT UP

Patty-cake, Patty-cake,
Violet Venable
Wanted the doctor to
Try without dread,

For the relief of her
Overanxiety,
Frontal lobotomy
On the wrong head.

CARTOON LOVE 1940-2010

In the nineteen forties, love is simple.
Boy, girl, boy, girl, boy, girl–
But no touching until you're engaged.
The boy is tall and broad shouldered.
The girl is blonde and unyielding.
The emotional scenes are about
Who is asking whom to the big dance.
Love means not doing it.
>   Guys never even know
>   That they're in the closet. The War
>   Leaves it all even more emphatic.
>   Long distance longing and not talking about
>   The hard edges of life. And
>   What happens abroad stays abroad. And
>   Then in the fifties no talking about
>   Anything at all important, anything at all.
Then suddenly in the late sixties
You can do new things out in public.
Sex, drugs, and light shows. Holding hands.
This War makes it all even more possible.
And it becomes a badge of honor
To be cool about relationships. Interracial
Sex. Group sex. Everybody in the pool!
Sex ed's required in junior high school.
>   And the tattoos go rolling along,
>   Marking time for us. Sailors. Biker gangs.
>   Men in prison. Women on the make.
>   Goths. Butch bottoms showing off.

Then ordinary guys. Then
Ordinary guys trying too hard.
Every man flashes a sleeve of tattoos
Climbing out across his chest.
Now we are adrift. Or have slipped away.
Divorce is a sacrament–
More common than martrimony.
Sex is required in junior high.
Little children use foul language
Out in the street. Girls too.
Nobody wants to get caught
Taking sex at all seriously.
   And every high school boy
   Aspires to be a male model.
   The workout routines.
   And the phone sex. And reality TV.
   And no relationships. And internet sex.
   So you can flaunt it in public.
   But with no commitments, thank you.
   Again war makes it even more urgent.
And gay marriage, check,
On the political agenda
While everybody's at the gym
And so in love with himself,
Texting sex seriously but never taking
The plunge. Hermetically sealed,
Nobody ever actually knows
Another person in person.

STRANGER

With lushness oozing out of me
like remontant roses from a wound
I round you right with smoke rings
and seduce the air we breathe
describing in particulars
the essence of vermouth.
But then I slowly lose it,
refill my glass with tears,
and crowd among the ice cubes
to melt another day.

NO GORILLA

Then one day you suddenly know
that you're not a gorilla
and there's no use pretending you are,
so you slouch in your seat
and you slouch when you stand
and go limp
in your dungarees.

THE ORANGE CHALLENGE

For Warren Beatty, in the hot seat
during Splendor in the Grass *and* The Roman Spring of Mrs. Stone
and then again during Dick Tracy *and* Truth or Dare

Although Madonna says he never has been manned,
      Once there was near surrender in the grass
      When William Inge flew a protégé first class
Down Puerto Villarta way, performance safely canned,
To introduce Him-of-th'Enormous-Thing
      To Tennessee in his orangery
      Seeking sunkissed liquidy mercen'ry
Rentier to juice up *The Roman Spring.*

Warren's tongue boldly proved Italianate.
Tennessee, feeling he had no need to wait,
Approved him, thinking—at some later date—
He would languidly reciprocate.
      But Warren never came across. No one, bar Inge,
      E'er again in splendor squeezed that orange.

TASTE IT

In your mouth
poetry tastes like
life.
Inside your body
prose lives.
We keep the hard Latin
in the refrigerator
while the easy Greek ripens
in sunlight.

EM

About the Author:

E dmund Miller, Senior Professor of English at LIU–Post and former long-term Department Chair, is most renowned for *The Go Go Boy Sonnets* but has published a dozen other poetry books and chapbooks. In addition, three of his plays are in verse: *The Greeks Have a Word* (a reconstructed satyr play), *Loving Cuckold* (in heroic couplets), and *Royal Favorite; or, Regime Change* (in blank verse). His short fiction is collected as *Night Times*. Miller also writes extensively about British literature and is the acknowledged authority on Lewis Carroll's *Sylvie and Bruno* books while his *Drudgerie Divine: The Rhetoric of God and Man in George Herbert* is the most comprehensive study of that author.

Major Works of Poetry and Fiction:

Nature's Nest of Boxes: A Book of Haiku. With Collage Illustrations by John Digby. Oyster Bay NY: Feral Press, 2014.

A Rider of Currents. With Collage Illustrations by John Digby. Oyster Bay NY: Feral, 2009.

The Go-Go Boy Sonnets: Men of the New York Club Scene. Portland OR: Inkwater, 2005.

Night Times. London: Zipper Imprint of Prowler, 2000.

Leavings. Northport NY: Birnham Wood, 1995.

The Happiness Cure; and, Other Poems. Northport NY: Birnham Wood, 1993.

Fucking Animals: A Book of Poems. 1973; Sarasota: Florida Literary Foundation, 1994.

Scholarly Books:

Editor with Tammy Nuzzo-Morgan, Peter Thabit Jones, Lynn E Cohen, and J R Turek. *Long Island Sounds IV.* Southampton: Wild Island, 2009.

Intro. and notes. *Stories Toto Told Me* by Baron Corvo. Chicago: Valancourt, 2008.

George Herbert's Kinships: An Ahnentafel with Annotations. Bowie MD: Heritage, 1993.

Editor with Robert DiYanni. *Like Season'd Timber: New Essays on George Herbert.* New York: Peter Lang, 1987.

Editor. *Mount Orgueil; or, Divine and Profitable Meditations* by William Prynne: *A Facsimile Edition.* Delmar: Scholars' Facsimiles & Reprints, 1984.

Drudgerie Divine: The Rhetoric of God and Man in George Herbert. Salzburg: Universität Salzburg, 1979.

Full-Length Plays Staged:

The Greeks Have a Word.
Royal Favorite; or, Regime Change.
The Colonel's Lady.
Loving Cuckold.
The Last Conquests of Beau Fersen; or, Boudoir Diplomacy.
Queen Christina in Exile; or, The Betrayal of Monaldeschi.

www.ingramcontent.com/pod-product-compliance
Lightning Source LLC
Chambersburg PA
CBHW032026090426
42741CB00006B/742